The Mystery of the Missing Mystery

Written by Marcia Vaughan
Illustrated by Beccy Blake

Rigby • Steck-Vaughn

www.steck-vaughn.com

Contents

		Page
Chapter 1	**Fogtop Is on the Case**	3
Chapter 2	**A Sneaky Elf**	8
Chapter 3	**The Sinking Ship**	12
Chapter 4	**The Chewed-Up Pencil**	18

Chapter 1  Fogtop Is on the Case

Ring! Ring!

Detective Fogtop's phone woke him from his nap. He picked up his calculator and put it to his ear. "Hello," he said. "How strange. Nobody's there."

Ring! Ring!

Detective Fogtop dropped the calculator and picked up the phone. "Hello," he said. "This is Detective Fogtop, mystery solver."

A voice on the phone said, "This is Rita Romero, the mystery writer. I need your help. Someone has stolen my new mystery story! Please come over right away."

"Don't worry, Miss Romero," Detective Fogtop said. "I'm on my way."

An hour later, Detective Fogtop knocked on the door of Rita Romero's grand house. Rita and her daughter, Maria, showed him into the library. Rita pointed to a fancy new computer sitting on a desk.

"I type my mysteries on this computer and save them on a floppy disk. My new story is called *The Mystery of the Sinking Ship*. When I came in this morning, the disk was gone! I printed a copy of the finished story last night, and that's gone, too.

"My story has to be ready for the Who-Done-It Publishing Company today. Violet Snippy, who works for the company, arrived earlier today," Rita said. "Violet wants to write about me for the local newspaper. She wants to be a writer, too, and I like to help young writers when I can. Violet has offered to take the mystery story to the publishing company when she has finished talking to me. Oh, what am I going to do?"

"Is anything else missing?" Detective Fogtop asked.

"Mother," Maria said, "your painting of the sinking ship is gone!"

Rita Romero looked at the wall above the fireplace. "Oh, no! That painting gave me the idea for my new mystery," she said.

Just then, Rita, Maria, and Detective Fogtop heard someone coming. "Oh, dear," Rita said. "There's Violet Snippy now. She thinks that my story is ready. I'd better tell her that it's been stolen." Rita left the library.

Chapter  A Sneaky Elf

Detective Fogtop began to pace back and forth, thinking hard.

"Watch out," Maria said, but she was too late. Detective Fogtop had already tripped over the footstool.

"Ouch!" he said, lying on the floor. Then he picked up a strange feathery object under the desk. "Oh, my! It's a rare ostrich tail. I guess the thief dropped it. From the amount of dust on it, I'd say it must be very old. It's clear that the thief collects rare and valuable things."

"It doesn't look like an ostrich tail to me. To me, it looks like a—" Maria started to say.

"Now, now," Detective Fogtop interrupted. "No time for chatter. I must look for more clues." Detective Fogtop put the ostrich tail in his pocket and sat down to think. "Ouch!" he said. There was a pointed tool in the chair. "Oh, my! It's a tiny shovel. Clearly, the mystery story was stolen by a sneaky elf who digs for rare and valuable ostrich tails."

"Are you sure?" asked Maria. "To me, that elf shovel looks more like a—"

"Now, now," Detective Fogtop said. "I know what I'm doing." He put the shovel in his pocket and looked on the desk.

"Is that a clue, too?" Maria said, pointing at a pencil with purple smears.

"That pencil won't help me with this case," said Detective Fogtop. "But it will be useful for taking notes later."

While Maria watched, Detective Fogtop sat down again. He started to make a list of all the elves he knew who collected rare objects. He couldn't think of one elf. Suddenly, he heard voices in the hall. Rita came into the library talking to a young woman with purple lipstick, a purple shirt, and purple pants.

"Your new mystery story is missing?" the young woman asked.

"Someone stole it this morning, Violet," said Rita sadly.

"Well, we need a new mystery story right away!" Violet snapped. "If you can't find your mystery, I'll write one myself!" She marched off, looking pleased with herself.

Chapter 3 The Sinking Ship

"Detective Fogtop, you really must find the thief and my missing mystery," Rita said. "It took me months to write it!"

"I already know who took it," said Detective Fogtop proudly. "After studying the clues, I am sure that the thief is an elf who collects rare and valuable things. Have you seen any elves in your library, Miss Romero?"

Rita looked confused. "An elf? I've never seen an elf."

"Then I'd better see if anyone else in the house has. I'll talk with the maid first." Detective Fogtop left Rita and Maria and went to find the maid.

Detective Fogtop rushed downstairs and got lost in the basement. Sometime later, he found the maid upstairs in a bedroom. Mildred Mildew was dusting furniture with her hands.

"Miss Mildew, I'm Detective Fogtop. I'm here to find Miss Romero's story and the thief who took it," Detective Fogtop said. "Have you seen an elf?"

"No," she said and began to laugh. "I've never seen an elf! Why do you want to know?"

"Because I found this rare ostrich tail at the scene of the crime," Detective Fogtop answered. "And I'm sure the thief is an elf who collects rare and valuable things."

Mildred Mildew grabbed the duster from Detective Fogtop and waved it over the furniture.

"What are you doing?" asked Detective Fogtop. "That is a valuable clue!"

"That is my feather duster," Mildred said. "I must have left it in the library."

"Oh, no," said Detective Fogtop. "Maybe the elf doesn't collect ostrich tails after all. The thief could be any elf! I'll have to find out more from the gardener."

Detective Fogtop rushed into the garden and got tangled up in the roses. Mr. Weed, Rita's gardener, came along and untangled him.

"Mr. Weed, I'm Detective Fogtop, and I'm here to find Miss Romero's story and the thief who took it," Detective Fogtop said. "Have you seen a sneaky elf running around?"

"No," said Mr. Weed. "I've been too busy digging holes in the garden with my hands."

"Never mind that," said Detective Fogtop.

"There's a sneaky elf on the loose around here!"

"An elf?" asked Mr. Weed. "I've never seen an elf here."

"I know all about the elf," Detective Fogtop said. "I found his tiny shovel at the scene of the crime."

Mr. Weed laughed. "That's no elf shovel! That's my gardening shovel—and I need it."

"Well, how did it get in the library?" Detective Fogtop asked.

"I was in the library taking the painting of the sinking ship," Mr. Weed said. "I think I left the shovel on a chair."

"I knew it!" shouted Detective Fogtop. "You're the thief, Mr. Weed!"

The gardener looked confused. "I didn't steal the painting," Mr. Weed said. "I knew that the painting was the idea behind Miss Romero's new mystery story. I took the painting so I could put a new frame on it. I was going to give it to Miss Romero as a surprise."

"Oh, dear," said Detective Fogtop, and he began to pace back and forth again. "I'm not a great mystery solver after all! I'd better go look for more clues!"

Chapter 4 The Chewed-Up Pencil

Detective Fogtop was walking up the steps of the front porch when the door burst open. A young woman clutching a paper bag dashed out the door. It was Violet Snippy. "Get out of my way!" she yelled.

But Detective Fogtop began to move the wrong way. Violet Snippy crashed into him. They both fell down the steps. Violet Snippy dropped her bag. All sorts of things fell out of Detective Fogtop's pockets.

"Look at what you've done!" Violet Snippy shouted. "And what are you doing with my pencil?"

Detective Fogtop looked surprised. "Are you sure this is your pencil?" he asked. "It was in my pocket."

"Yes, I'm sure," Miss Snippy said. "It has my purple lipstick on it. I chew my pencils when I'm thinking. Where did you get it?"

"I found it at the scene of the crime," Detective Fogtop answered. "But it's not a clue. You can have it back."

Violet Snippy grabbed the pencil and jumped to her feet. Detective Fogtop tried to help her. He reached for the paper bag at the same time as she did.

"Give that to me!" Violet shouted, pulling the paper bag so hard that it ripped open. A floppy disk dropped to the ground. Sheets of paper sailed through the air. Violet began to grab them.

Detective Fogtop felt foolish. Everything he had thought was wrong. He hadn't solved the mystery at all.

Hearing all the noise, Rita and Maria came to the door. Rita came down the ramp on the porch. Maria hurried to help Violet pick up the sheets of paper. She picked up a sheet of paper and handed it to Detective Fogtop. "Look at this," she said.

Detective Fogtop read the first two lines out loud: *"The Mystery of the Sinking Ship* by Rita Romero."

"Is that my missing mystery?" Rita asked.

"Yes, this is it," said Detective Fogtop. "Violet Snippy had it all the time!"

Rita looked at Violet Snippy in surprise. "Why did you take my story?"

Violet Snippy hung her head. "The Who-Done-It Publishing Company wanted to publish a new mystery. I hoped that if your story was not ready, they would publish my mystery story instead," she said. "Now I guess I'll lose my job. And I'm not really going to write about you for my local newspaper. I just wanted to ask you how to write a good mystery. I'm sorry," she muttered.

"I'm sorry you're going to lose your job, Miss Snippy," Rita said. "But you will have more free time now. Maybe you can use the time to write."

"I guess I can," said Violet in a small voice.

"If you work hard, you might get a story published," Rita said.

Violet Snippy's eyes lit up. "Do you really think so?"

"Yes, if it's good enough," Rita told her.

Rita turned to the detective. "Thank you, Detective Fogtop, for everything you've done," she said. "I think you are the best detective in the world."

"Thank you, Miss Romero. I'm very proud of being a mystery solver. As a matter of fact, I have solved another mystery," Detective Fogtop went on. He put a hand on Mr. Weed's shoulder. "I know who stole your painting. It's going to be a shock."

But no one was listening to him.